Excellent!

... This book is clear and concise, and very readable and helpful. Everyone can benefit from it. It deals with things you know in the back of your mind, like when to hand out your business card, or how to escape from a conversation gracefully. We all encounter these situations, and they are most relevant.

—Julie Wade, Sales Representative, Pearson Education

I enjoyed this book very much. It is easy to read, and very practical. It touches on various aspects of making a first impression. It would be very helpful for anyone starting a career, as well as a refresher for someone who has been in business for a while, and just forgot certain things. The book is compact and interesting. I wanted to learn more about the subject. I would recommend it to friends who are professionals or self-employed, or just coming out of school and starting a career.

—Angela Di Virgilio, Attorney

How to Make a Million Dollar First Impression offers practical, no-nonsense tips that you can use immediately to give you the edge on the competition.

—Andrei Pancu, Software Engineer, Peernet Inc.

This is a comprehensive instructional book on business etiquette—excellent for people who are just starting out and want some general tips for success. It is clear, concise and to the point, easy to read and understand. I like the quotes from people who are actually dealing with applicants.

—Omer Mendelson, McGill University student

This book is a great resource for university and college grads looking for their first job. Entering the workforce for the first time is stressful. Knowing proper business etiquette can give you that added confidence needed to land that first job. More specifically, the book will be great for students that haven't studied business and had experience with networking and interactions with business professionals.

—Jane Ngo, Queens University student

In this age of instant money, many assume they have instant prestige. However, class is learned, not earned. This book teaches those of us who think we know, and those whom many of us think should know, some basic rules of etiquette. There are not many people, executives or otherwise, who will not pick up some essential tips for courtesy in meeting people, whether it is for business or at a charitable event. How to Make a Million Dollar First Impression reminds us all of basic courtesy, and will help those who follow it stand out in a crowd.

—Stephanie Black, VP, People Communications
Media Trainer/Communications Consultant

How to Make a Million Dollar First Impression

Lynda Goldman

GSBC

GSBC

Contact:
Lynda Goldman
2216 Mediterranée
St-Laurent, Quebec
Canada H4R 3B1
Tel.: (514) 336-4339
Fax :(514) 336-9805
E-mail : Lynda@impressforsuccess.com
www.impressforsuccess.com

Canadian Cataloguing in Publishing Data

Goldman, Lynda, Date –
How to Make a Million Dollar First Impression

Includes Index
ISBN 0-9694996-1-2

Success in business. 2. Business etiquette.
I. Smythe, Sandra, Date – II. Title

HF5389.G64 2000 650.1 C00-900532-3

Cover design by Monica Kompter
Layout by Wendi Petersen, Éditique Bunbury

Printed and bound in Canada

Fifth printing

Acknowledgments

Wc would likc to acknowlcdgc and thank cveryone who gave us input, suggestions and quotes for this book. Your contributions and feedback were invaluable in shaping this book. Our many thanks go to:

Mark Berkowitz, Stephanie Black, Ian Blair, Andrea Bruderer, Alice Bohdjalian, Diane Bussandri, Lorraine Byrne, Douglas Cameron, Michel Daigle, Micheline Daoust, Dany Dépatie, Joe Dicso, Angela Di Virgilio, Max Goldman, Millicent Goldman, Rick Goldman, Robert Lee, Diane Lefebvre, Marie Malo, Steve Manning, Omer Mendelson, Marshall Moreyne, Jane Ngo, Sean O'Shea, Andrei Pancu, Sonia Pehlivanian, Wendi Petersen, Sandra Roscanu, Martin Shaw, Andrea Strom-Rancourt, Tom Stoyan, Mireille Tanguay, Gabrielle Thibaudeau, Alvaro Trueba, Sandy Thompson, Julie Wade

How to Make a Million Dollar First Impression

Dear Reader,

Where are you now in your career path? Are you about to embark on a career change? Are you working towards a promotion or looking for a job? Are you in customer service, sales or marketing? Are you looking for clients for your business? Wherever you are, you'll be in contact with people who can influence your career. The impression you make on them will have an impact – one way or the other.

Making a million dollar first impression won't get you the job or the promotion you want, immediately. That's not what the first impression is for. A great first impression opens the door, so that you can make a second impression, and then a third. Each time you will reinforce and build on your positive first impression. This is how you really get to show your talents and abilities. This is where people get to know the real you.

But here's the catch. Without a great first impression, you may never get to make that second impression. So we can say the first impression is the key. Once you learn how to make a great first impression, you can use these tools all the time – easily and simply. The habits you learn will become second nature to you. For example, once you learn the powerful effects of making eye contact, you won't have to think twice about it. It will be something you do automatically.

This book is organized into powerful one-minute lessons. Each idea is on a separate page, so you can read the book from front to back, or just the pages that will help you the most. The ideas will give you tools to help you. These tools are condensed into "golden nuggets."

Use this book along your career path. Carry the book with you. Give it as a gift to friends. Refer to it whenever you're in a new business situation. Polish your skills so that you present your best self to the world. Then you will reach your personal and business goals.

—Lynda and Sandra

Table of Contents

Part 1

We all have an image—what's yours?

It is only shallow people
who do not judge
by appearances.
—Oscar Wilde

1. How the right tools and preparation can help you reach your goals

Have you ever been in a business situation where you felt uncertain? Have you been promoted to a position that needed more people skills than you have? Do your best qualities really come through at job interviews?

We all feel discomfort in new situations. Take Laurie P., for example. Laurie, a 26-year-old woman, had worked in sales for several years when her company closed. She heard about a job opening in a publishing company. Laurie loved books and thought this would be her ideal job. But when she found out that the interview would be with the president of the division, she became nervous.

Laurie asked us to help her prepare for the interview. We helped her select a suit and accessories. Laurie practiced a firm handshake, and worked on her body language. She prepared for the interview by learning about the company, and by presenting the right image—and she got the job. Afterwards she told us how much the preparation had helped her. Laurie learned how to present a professional image. This gave her the confidence she needed to land her dream job. With the same tools, you can reach your goals too.

2. Why we think in images, and how this is important to you

Meet Kathryn Brown—quick-witted, cautious, workaholic. Meet Joe Green—easy-going, friendly, know-it-all. What springs to your mind? Which person is more likely to succeed in business? Which person would you like to work with?

How did you answer these questions? Based on only three descriptive words, you formed an image in your mind. Why? Because we make judgments based on image. Every person, product, place and business has an image. What image comes to mind when you think of New York? Is it the same as Tahiti? Why do we associate hot dogs with baseball, and escargots with French restaurants? Why would anyone want to taste snails in the first place, if not for their image as sophisticated food?

We all project an image. Have you thought about the image you project? If not, that may be exactly what people see—an image of non-awareness. Isn't it better to take charge of your image, so you project the positive traits that are truly inside you?

If you come across as unprofessional in the first five seconds of a job interview, it will cost you the rest of the interview. It is possible to overcome an initial bad impression, but it's difficult. Why put yourself at that disadvantage?

—Lorraine Byrne, Human Resources Manager, SF Marketing

At a job interview, many people don't realize they are there to sell themselves. They arrive wearing sneakers, or dressed inappropriately. They are not prepared. They don't know anything about the company. They don't ask the proper questions, so they look like they are just looking for a salary. They become too familiar when they should be more formal. It's like trying to do a good presentation with no tools.

—Dany Depatie, Human Resources Manager, Dynacast Canada Inc.

3. The reason we make quick judgments, and why this is important to know

Did you know that you have ten seconds to make a lasting first impression? Albert Mehrabian, a UCLA psychologist, conducted experiments that revealed how people perceive each other. He found that first impressions are based on the following criteria:

- 55 percent is visual
- 38 percent is for our voices
- 7 percent is for what we say

Clearly our visual image is the most important. People size each other up at a glance!

You may be saying, "That's not fair. People should get to know the real me." It may not be fair, but it's the way the world works. In business, people don't have time to get to know the *real* you. People make quick judgments, and they seldom change their minds. You may be saying that it's the product inside that counts. That's true. But if you never pick up the package, you'll never have the valuable product inside. Anyone in package design knows this. We are visual creatures. That's why the package is often designed before the product!

golden nugget 1 — Your physical appearance is your visual resume.

4. Why the "silent signals" you send are vital to your career

Our visual impression is made up of five things: the clothes we wear, our body language, our facial expressions, our posture, and our gestures. These are the "silent signals" we send into the room.

At a job interview or networking event you can say all the right things. But a frown on your face, or clothes that belong at the beach will undo all your well-planned words.

The image we present speaks volumes about us. When you wear your best business suit, stand tall and speak with enthusiasm, you have the winning edge. You are more likely to succeed than someone with equal qualifications, but less professional presence.

Surveys show that people with professional presence and communication skills are more likely to get the jobs they want. They are also promoted more quickly and command higher salaries. Shouldn't you make your visual image work for you?

5. Why understanding your business role is crucial to creating the right image

The business world is a kind of theatre. You may be working with the public or winning clients for your company. You may be preparing for a job interview or a promotion. You have to understand your role, so you can decide how to act and how to present yourself.

Within minutes of meeting someone we make assumptions about many different aspects of their personalities: age, education, economic status, marital status, occupation, trustworthiness and likelihood of success.

Think about who you are, and your role in the business world. Kathryn, applying for a job in an investment firm, needs to project trustworthiness in her image. She needs a conservative suit and accessories. Joe, working in an advertising agency, would look out of place in a navy blue suit. He looks creative and up-to-date by wearing trendy clothes. Robert, working in the high-tech industry, wears casual clothes every day.

What's your role? What qualities do you want to project?

The initial few minutes of an interview are the key. When you walk into a job interview well dressed and give a firm handshake, you will make a strong first impression. The first impression is for information gathering. That will influence whether you have a chance to make a second impression.

—Martin Shaw, Executives Available

Part 2

What do people see when they look at you?

I've always wanted
to be somebody.
But I can see now
I should have been
more specific.
—Lily Tomlin

6. What your face reveals about you and what you can do about it

Have you ever gotten the wrong signals from someone? Maybe your friend looks upset, and you ask, "What's wrong?" Your friend answers, "Nothing. I was just thinking about something."

We are often unaware of our facial expressions. We think our expression shows concentration, but to others it looks like a frown. A furrowed brow makes us look anxious or angry, even if our words are positive. Many business people cultivate a poker face, hoping not to reveal anything when they are negotiating. This may work well at the negotiating table, but not so well in other circumstances.

UCLA psychologist Albert Mehrabian's experiments showed that our facial expression has more impact than our voice or words. If you are not sure of how your facial expressions come across, look in a mirror, or ask a friend.

golden nugget 2 Of all the things you wear, your facial expression is the most important.

7. Why a genuine smile has a powerful impact

We may not all be naturally beautiful, but we can all look better instantly with the most inexpensive cosmetic of all—a smile. Smiling may seem obvious, but it's not as simple as it seems. We tend to continue the habits we formed in childhood, so some men need to smile more, while some women should be careful not to over-smile.

False smiles are not beautiful. They involve only the lips, rather than the whole face. Don't smile or grin when you are giving or receiving bad news. Your facial expression should match the situation.

When you have a genuine smile, you show friendliness and interest in others. Your smile conveys warmth and openness. It inspires confidence, and draws positive attention to you. Smiles make others feel at ease, and are instant energizers. A genuine smile is not just with your lips. There is an old saying, "Smile with your eyes."

> Smile, smile, smile.
>
> **—Mireille Tanguay, Manager,**
> **Customer Relations and Personal Shopping, Birks**

8. Why eye contact gives you "eye communication"

Making eye contact shows that you are focused on other people. It's the best way to show that you are listening to what they are saying. In fact, in western cultures, if you aren't looking at the speaker, he or she will assume you aren't paying attention. People who make eye contact are considered trustworthy. Unfortunately, shy people who avert their eyes may be thought of as shifty. Don't go to the extreme of staring at someone's face, however.

Here are three tips for communicating with your eyes:

- Look at the person's entire face rather than staring into their eyes.
- Watch their lips when they speak. This helps you "hear" what they're saying.
- Break the tension of uninterrupted eye contact by occasionally jotting down some information, or by gazing over the person's shoulder from time to time.

9. How your body language sends out silent messages

Have you ever noticed how politicians enter a room? They stride confidently to the podium. They move purposefully. They control their motions. Politicians are keenly aware of how body movement affects their image.

Your body language sends out a message about you—before you say a word. Ted, a 30-year-old computer technician, was looking for a new job. He attended a networking event for the high-tech industry. He went into the room with his chin down and avoided eye contact with anyone. He was hoping someone would approach him and start a conversation. Of course, no one did. He was sending a clear signal that he was uncomfortable and anxious.

Bonnie, a 29-year-old systems analyst, was at the same event. She paused in the doorway, and then walked purposefully into the room. Her posture and manner said, "I'm here. I know what I'm supposed to do." She made some valuable contacts at that event.

When you enter a room, pause long enough to get your bearings. Then walk with enthusiasm and confidence towards your destination. A slow, deep, purposeful nod, a smile, and a relaxed facial expression show your confidence and poise in any situation.

10. How standing tall helps you face the world head on

Deborah H. is a tall woman—close to six feet tall. She stands up even when others sit down. "When I was younger, I used to slouch to hide my height," she said. "Now I stand up straight. I appear confident and in control—even when I don't feel that way inside."

Yes, your mother told you to stand up straight. Slouching makes you appear tired or sloppy. People who hang their heads appear shy and withdrawn, or defeated. Criminals know that people who walk slowly or tentatively are easy victims.When you stand up straight, not only do you look better, you feel more confident.

Our culture expects business people to be level-headed, to think clearly and rationally. Standing tall makes it easier to look others in the eye and maintain eye contact.

Stand with your feet parallel to your hips and shoulders. Avoid swaying or shifting from side to side. Be careful about crossing your legs at the ankles when you stand. It puts you off balance. Stand straight and face people head on.

11. How your mannerisms can make you the center of attention—for the wrong reasons

At a department meeting, Julie begins to yawn and glance at her watch. Mike jiggles the keys in his pocket and taps his foot. Julie and Mike are not aware of how their small gestures come across, but others are.

We all feel tired, bored or distracted at times, but we may not realize how our mannerisms come across. We chew our fingernails, play with our hair or scratch various parts of the body. We fiddle with paper clips or click our pens.

If you chew gum, smoke, or suck on candy in a meeting, you aren't projecting a professional image. When you make an effort to control our body language, you appear calm and relaxed.

Julie and Mike are sending messages that they are tired and bored. Tune in to your mannerisms and think about the messages you send. We can "catch" ourselves, and eliminate distracting habits so we look poised and professional. Ask a trusted friend to help you identify your tics and twitches.

golden nugget 3 Your body language speaks louder than the words you say.

Someone with a good smile shows he or she has gusto. At a job interview, a smile makes you look happy to be there and as if you want the job. You've broken through one of the barriers, and this makes it seem as if you're already part of the team.

—Micheline Daoust, Director of Training and Development, Quantum

Part 3

How to generate warm feelings when you meet people

Charm is the ability to make
someone else think that
both of you
are wonderful.
—Edgar Magnin

12. Why your handshake is a key element of your business image

Diane and Nick, two colleagues, are waiting for a meeting to begin. When the manager enters the room, Nick stands up and shakes hands. Diane remains seated. During the meeting, the manager asks Nick's opinion more frequently than he asks Diane's. Diane tries to contribute her comments, but somehow she doesn't feel that the manager is really listening to her.

Make a strong first impression by being the first to extend your hand. Business is about being in control. The person who extends a hand first has the advantage. This is true for women as well as for men. A handshake is appropriate in each of these situations:

- When you are introduced to someone
- When you say goodbye to someone
- At the beginning and end of a meeting
- In any appropriate business situation

Some people may seem uncomfortable about shaking hands—for cultural reasons, for example. In that case, simply acknowledge the person with a smile and a nod.

golden nugget 4 Extend your hand to anyone you are doing business with—male or female.

13. How to make your hand-to-hand contact a shake of power

Have you ever shaken hands with someone who squeezes your hand so hard you want to scream, "Stop!" How about with someone who weakly clasps your fingers and shakes them? We've all experienced a variety of handshakes. Some of them are memorable, but for the wrong reasons.

It's easy to have a winning handshake, and the payoff is great. A firm handshake shows that you have confidence, power and authority. To give a memorable handshake:

1. Extend your hand straight, not palm up or palm down.

2. Clasp the other person's hand firmly. The webs between your thumbs and forefingers should meet.

3. Shake firmly once or twice and then let go. Don't keep pumping up and down.

Use the power of the handshake to build trust and show respect. Your handshake is the first, and only, physical contact you have in business. It "starts the clock," on your first impression. Make it a great one!

14. How to create positive feelings with your greeting

Have you ever met someone and immediately liked him or her? Have you ever instantly disliked someone you met? We form these feelings in a flash, based on the small details of a greeting.

Richard sees Tom sitting at a table at a meeting, and goes over to introduce himself. He extends his hand and says, “Hello. I’m Richard. Nice to meet you.” Tom responds with, “Yeah, likewise.” Tom remains seated, so Richard has to lean over to shake hands. That puts him, and their business relationship, a little off balance.

Next, Richard goes over to Joe, sitting at another table. When Richard introduces himself, Joe stands up, smiles, looks Richard in the eyes, and says, “I’m pleased to meet you too.” They are off to a great start.

When you meet someone new, step towards the person, smile, make eye contact, and greet him or her warmly. If you are sitting, stand up so you are both at eye level. Introduce yourself by saying something like, “I’m pleased to meet you.” Most likely, the other person will respond genuinely by saying, “I’m happy to meet you too!”

15. How a smooth self-introduction can open up the conversation

Imagine you are being introduced to someone. You each say your name, shake hands, and say something like, "Nice to meet you." Now what do you do? You feel awkward with this new acquaintance, and fumble around trying to think of what to say next.

You can make your greetings much smoother by planning a clear and interesting introduction. Practice your introduction in front of a mirror until you feel comfortable with it. Offer some information about yourself that will help you start a conversation. For example, you can say,

"Hello. I'm Carol Jones. I'm an accountant with ABC Company. I help people manage and save their money."

"Hello. I'm Tom Martin. My company, XYZ, designs computer software to help small businesses."

Now Tom can ask Carol about the accounting field, ABC Company, or managing money. Carol can ask Tom about XYZ Company, and about the kind of software he designs and how it helps small businesses. Your introduction can lead to some interesting discussion.

16. An easy rule to use when you introduce people

You're at a business cocktail party, talking with a colleague. You see your client coming towards you. Whom do you name first in the introduction? What happens when your boss approaches?

The rule is easy to remember. Rank is more important than gender. Say the name of the person with the most authority or importance first. For example, "Steve Jones, (your client), this is Jane White, my colleague." Remember that clients may not fit into your company hierarchy, but they are certainly very important. When introducing your boss, you can say, "Mr. Smith, I'd like you to meet Jane White."

If you are not sure who has more importance, you can fall back on tradition. Say the name of the older person, or the woman, first. For example, "Steve Forty, this is Bill Thirty," or "Jane, this is Steve."

Remember to look at each person as you make the introduction. First look at the person with higher authority. Then look at the other person you are introducing.

golden nugget 5

Say the name of the most honored person first in business introductions. Remember that the client is always the most important person in a business relationship.

Part 4

The name game and why it's so important

There is no sound so sweet
as the sound
of one's own name.
—William Shakespeare

17. The most important word you should use, and why

Every morning a line of people snakes around the corner at the coffee shop where Jessica works. People patiently wait for Jessica to serve them before they head off to their offices. The coffee here is good, but it's not any better than the coffee next door. What's the secret of the long line up? Jessica greets each customer by name. She usually remembers who takes extra cream or sugar, and who likes cappuccino. She makes each customer feel special.

When someone takes the trouble to learn and remember your name, you feel special. You think highly of that person, because he or she makes you feel valued.

When you are introduced in a business setting, give the person your full attention, and repeat his or her name. You can say something like, "Nice to meet you, Ms White." Use the person's last name until you are invited to do otherwise. Don't ask if you can use the person's first name. He or she will be sure to let you know when to do this.

golden nugget 6 Use someone's name to show you value them.

18. How to keep peoples' names from going in one ear and out the other

What happens after we hear someone's name for the first time? A moment later our minds go blank, and we can't remember the name. This happens because we feel nervous during an introduction. We are focusing on ourselves, and the kind of impressions we are making.

The key is to focus on the other person. Repeat the name as soon as you hear it, and try to visualize it written down. Use the name in the introduction. "It's nice to meet you, Mr. Adams." If you repeat the name three times in the course of a conversation, you will probably remember it.

You can help the other person remember your name by saying it slowly and clearly. You know your own name, so you may say it quickly. Instead, pause after your first name. Say, "Hello, my name is Carol (pause) Jones." Smile when you introduce yourself. Look happy to meet the person.

If your name is unusual or difficult to pronounce, help the person out by spelling it, or writing it down for them. You can smile and say, "I know it's a tough one," but don't make a big deal out of it.

19. Why using the correct name and job title is crucial

David is introducing Patricia, his colleague, to a client. He says, "Jim, this is Pat. We work together in accounting." Patricia wonders who "Pat" is. She doesn't know anyone by that name.

There is nothing as irritating as having someone call you by the wrong name. If someone is called Patricia, don't shorten her name to Pat. If you hear someone else call her Pat, you can ask her which name she prefers. Everyone wants to hear his or her own name, and to have it pronounced correctly.

Be sure to use the correct job title as well. A senior vice-president should not be addressed as "vice-president," and an administrative assistant does not appreciate being called a secretary. We are all sensitive about how we are acknowledged. Paying attention to rank and job title is crucial to making a great first impression.

20. How to rescue people when they can't remember your name

You're greeting someone you haven't seen in a while. You say, "Hi Jeffrey, how are you?" Jeffrey is looking at you with an embarrassed expression. You realize he's forgotten your name.

When someone can't remember your name, come to the rescue quickly. Just extend your hand, smile, and say your name. For example, "Hi. I'm Julie Smith. We met a few months ago." Don't act as if someone should remember your name, or ask, "Do you remember me?" It will only make them feel awkward.

If you have forgotten someone's name, don't make a big deal out of it. It happens to everyone. Simply say something like, "I'm sorry. Your name slipped my mind. Please tell me again." If you can remember the circumstances where you met, you can say, "I remember we met at the high-tech job fair last April, but I've forgotten your name at the moment."

All the people I knew in Mexico had Spanish names. When I first came to Canada, I often had trouble with names. People have so many languages; you hear a lot of unfamiliar names. I've learned to ask people to repeat their names, and even to spell them. I always check to see if I'm saying the name correctly. People appreciate that I take the trouble to get their name right.

—Alvaro Trueba, Entrepreneur

Part 5

Business basics that make you look savvy

Nothing succeeds like the
appearance of success.
—Christopher Lasch

21. Opening gambits: how to make your first words count

Kathryn is waiting for a job interview. When the interviewer greets her, she offers her hand and says, "Thank you for taking the time to see me, Mr. Williams." Mr. Williams is impressed, and the interview is off to a good start.

You can open a conversation easily and effectively with a compliment or a word of thanks. When you meet someone for the first time, thank them for meeting you. Include their name in your opening words whenever possible. For example,

- "It's a pleasure to meet you, Ms Green."
- "Thanks for suggesting we meet today, Mr. Smith."
- "It's great to see you again, Allison."

When you meet someone in his or her office, you can also make a positive comment about the décor or the location. For example, "You have a great view of the city from your window, Judy," or, "What a great location. It's right in the heart of downtown."

Be careful you don't say anything too personal, though. Avoid comments about the way the person looks or acts, or comments about other people in the workplace.

22. How you can avoid personal space wars

Tony and Fred are talking together after a business meeting. As Tony inches closer to Fred, Fred inches backwards. They are heading towards the wall. Has this ever happened to you?

We all have different comfort levels with physical space. North Americans generally stand at arms length, or about three feet apart, during a business conversation. In other cultures people may stand closer, or farther apart.

We use our personal space to show how we feel. We stand back when we feel upset or repelled by something. When you stand too far away from someone, the person may think you are "standoffish." When someone moves into your personal space you may feel they are trying to be too intimate.

You look professional when you keep an appropriate distance between you and the other person. If you notice he or she is backing away from you, resist the impulse to move closer. Perhaps you are standing in his or her comfort zone.

23. How the business and social worlds are different

Marie, an analyst, is headed towards the door with Robert, her manager. Who opens the door? Is it Robert, because he's the man, or Marie, the junior team member?

In a social situation, you would feel comfortable knowing that the man opens the door for a woman. But the business world today is gender neutral. We treat men and women the same way, and we expect them to act the same way.

If you aren't sure what to do, use common sense. Whoever gets to the door first opens it. Sometimes the man will fall back on tradition and hold the door open.

Whatever happens, you can be gracious about it. A man or woman can help someone struggling with his or her coat, or open a door for someone carrying a package. Whoever is closest to a revolving door or an elevator door enters or exits first.

Follow the same rules for men and women in today's gender-neutral business arena.

24. How someone you meet on the elevator can help you on the way up

Have you met the "elevator hog"? The elevator hog presses the button repeatedly while waiting for the elevator. When the elevator arrives, the elevator hog rushes in, blocking the exit. Then the elevator hog stands in front of the buttons so other people can't reach them. On the way up, the elevator hog is oblivious to people trying to get on or off the elevator.

You may feel anonymous in an elevator, but your next employer, client or colleague may be standing next to you. The elevator is a public place, and close encounters leave an impression.

Whether you are going up forty stories or down two floors, elevator etiquette is easy, and it makes the ride more pleasant. All you have to do is be aware of what's going on. Stand aside to let others enter and exit. If you are near the front of a crowded elevator, offer to push the buttons for others. Remember to say "excuse me" or "thank you" as others move to accommodate you. It's just common courtesy, and you never know who you'll encounter on the way up!

On the Team Canada Mission the Prime Minister of Canada and the ten premiers all made eye contact, gave genuine smiles and greeted us warmly.

—Robert Lee, Director of International Services, Eicon Technology

A businesswoman who impressed me had a strong warm handshake, direct gaze, a convincing smile, and gave an impression of self-assurance and openness to others.

—Diane Lefebvre, President of Diane Lefebvre Inc.

Part 6

Your image on paper announces who you are

I will prepare and someday
my chance will come.
—Abraham Lincoln

25. The small card that gives people five ways to reach you

You've just met some interesting people at a convention, and want to know how to reach them. You can write their names and numbers on a piece of paper or a napkin, of course. But isn't it much more convenient to exchange business cards?

Think of everything a business card does for you. It gives your name, company name and job title. And it gives as many as five ways to reach you: your address, phone number, fax number, e-mail address, and cell-phone number.

If you are in business, you should have a business card. Your information should be up-to-date and easy to read, with your name printed clearly. Keep a supply of business cards available. Make sure the cards you hand out are not torn, tattered or curled at the edges.

If your card has a lot of information on it, you may end up reducing the type size until it is nearly invisible. Be kind to people over forty who may need glasses for small print. Consider using the back of the card, or using a fold-over card to include all the information.

26. What your business card says about you

What image does your business card convey? Sophistication? Creativity? Trust? Does it tell people you are one of a kind, or one of many?

Your business card is the graphic symbol of your image. Think about how you want to be perceived. Your business card should show people who you are, and what kind of business you are in. For example, lawyers or financial planners often choose paper that looks like marble, to show a strong foundation. If you are in a creative field, an offbeat color or design will set you apart.

Your business card is your calling card. It gives basic information about how to reach you. But more important, it is part of the impression you make. An interesting logo and design compliment your image. Design your card so people will want to keep it.

golden nugget 8

Your business card represents your professional image. Make sure it's a "keeper."

Most people don't realize how important a business card is. They don't want to invest in a quality card, but the return on investment is great. A lot of business is through referral. A well-designed business card backs up your image.

Ninety-five percent of business cards are bland and boring. When you put some thought into your design, it puts you in the top five percent. You can work with a designer or enlist a creative friend to help you. Choose a different kind of paper or unusual typeface, or design a logo. People will keep your card, and remember you at the right time.

—Joe Dicso, Omni Serve

27. Exchanging business cards: how to be tactful, not tacky

At a networking event, John approaches a group, introduces himself, and starts handing out business cards as if they were sticks of chewing gum. People put the cards in their pockets, thinking, "This guy doesn't have much class."

Your business cards have value. Give them to people who ask for them, and are likely to use them. Otherwise people will just throw them out. You look tacky when you hand them out to everyone in a group because it looks as if you are trying to sell something.

Don't thrust your card on someone, particularly someone senior to you. If a senior person wants your card, he or she will ask for it. To ask for someone's business card, you can say, "How can I reach you?" rather than, "Can I have your business card?" If you want to make sure someone has your business card, try saying, "May I give you my business card?" instead of, "Here's my card."

When you receive a business card, don't just shove it into your pocket. Take a moment to look at it. Compliment the logo or design, say the person's name out loud, or comment on the location of his or her business. People will be delighted when you show interest in them.

All the world's a stage and most of us are desperately unrehearsed.

—Sean O'Casey

Laying the groundwork for your million dollar image

It is as hard to see one's self
as to look backwards without
turning around.
—Henry David Thoreau

28. How to speak so you don't, like, sound ditsy

Recently a young job candidate said to an interviewer, "You're, like, the marketing manager, aren't you?" The marketing manager replied, "I'm not "like" the marketing manager. I *am* the marketing manager."

Does your language make you sound like a high-school student hanging out at a shopping mall? Do you use "filler" words such as "like" without realizing it? Fillers and high-school jargon make you sound unprofessional. So does sloppy language such as "you guys" instead of "you," or "yeah" instead of "yes."

You can upgrade your language by consciously focusing on what you say. Sloppy language makes you look less credible, no matter how many degrees you have, or how you dress. You might want to work with a friend, to remind each other when you use fillers or unprofessional language.

29. How to be organized so you look confident, not confused

Janet rushes into a meeting with a new client. She is out of breath and her hair is flying out of its clip. She misplaced her papers, and had to search for them at the last minute. This nearly made her late for her appointment. The client's first impression of her is, "This woman seems disorganized. I wonder if she's right for my project?"

Before a business appointment, job interview, or cocktail party, take a few minutes to prepare. Organize your papers or résumé. Put your business cards in the pocket of your jacket, or another place when you can access them easily. Keep a pen and notebook within easy reach. Knowing that everything is at your fingertips will save you time, and you'll avoid fumbling or searching for things while under pressure.

Be organized in your thoughts as well. Think about the purpose for your meeting, and your desired outcome. Do you want to schedule a follow-up meeting, make a new contact, or connect with someone in particular?

Focus on the reason for your meeting, and plan ahead both physically and mentally. You will look and feel more confident and relaxed, and accomplish more as well.

30. How to master your timing to show good judgment

Mitchell is an overachiever. He has a job interview at 10:00. To make sure he's on time, he leaves home early, and arrives at his appointment at 9:35. As he waits in the reception area, the manager who will interview him looks up from his office across the hall. He notices Mitchell waiting. Mitchell sees the manager look at his watch in annoyance.

We all know that arriving late for an appointment is rude. It implies that your time is more valuable than the other person's. Not everyone is aware, however, that arriving too early isn't courteous either.

Business people are often rushed for time. They may be trying to meet a deadline, or return a phone call between appointments. When you arrive too early, the interviewer may feel pressured to see you right away. The best time to arrive is five to ten minutes before your meeting is scheduled.

Knowing when to leave is important too. When the meeting is arranged, you can ask approximately how long it will be. When the person you are meeting with looks at his or her watch, thanks you for your time, or starts to stand, conclude the meeting graciously and leave.

31. How to avoid making a bad impression at someone's office

Paul has an appointment with Mr. Callahan for an important contract. As he waits in the reception area, Paul pulls out a mystery novel and begins to read. Ten minutes later he sees a pair of shoes beside him, and realizes that Mr. Callahan is standing over him. Paul is completely engrossed in his book and hasn't seen Mr. Callahan approach.

Paul follows Mr. Callahan into his office, and plops himself down on the nearest chair. Mr. Callahan frowns. Paul puts his briefcase on Mr. Callahan's desk, and spreads his papers out.

Paul learns the hard way how not to act. He realizes, too late, that you should wait until someone indicates where to sit in their office. He also finds out that it's not a good idea to invade someone's personal space with your papers or briefcase. And he learns, after spilling coffee on the desk, that when you are nervous, it's a good idea not to take a cup of coffee, even if it's offered. He also learns not to grab candies from someone's desk unless they are offered, or to chew gum or take out a cigarette in someone's office. Poor Paul. His meeting was all downhill. Next time, he'll get it right.

One individual who came for a job interview was not paying attention to me. Although she was answering my questions, her eyes were darting all over, checking things in my office. This was a complete turn-off. Another individual pulled a chair close to my desk and tried to look at what I was writing.

At a job interview, you're trying to sell yourself. The way you sit, your eye contact, your grooming and politeness all contribute to your professionalism. Your first impression is very important."

—Sonia Pehlivanian, Human Resources Manager
Eutectic Canada Inc.

A man wrapped up in himself makes a very small package.

—Anonymous

32. How planning ahead for a meeting pays off

Andrea has a job interview on Thursday. A few days before, she calls the company to ask the receptionist's name, and find out about the dress code. She also asks where she can park her car. She arrives at 9:55, relaxed and confident.

Andrea greets the secretary by name, and gives her name. "Good morning Ms Sanders, I'm Andrea Sax. I have an appointment with Ms Johnson at 10:00." She hands the secretary her business card.

While she waits for Ms Johnson, Andrea reads the company information on the table. When Ms Johnson arrives, Andrea stands up, introduces herself and shakes hands.

During the meeting, Andrea sits up straight in her chair and maintains eye contact with Ms Johnson. She has planned ahead for the types of questions she would be asked, and has well-prepared answers. After the meeting, Andrea sends Ms Johnson a note of thanks for the time she took to meet with her. A week later Andrea gets the job she wanted. Her preparation paid off.

If my boss calls, get his name.

—Anonymous

Part 8

How to use clothes and accessories to create your visual image

Know yourself, then
create yourself.
—Mary McFadden

33. How your clothes can make people remember your face

Stephanie, a marketing manager in her early thirties, always looks well put-together. Her clothes are understated, but they are in style, and they suit her. Bonnie, her colleague in the sales department, tries to follow the latest trends, but she never looks quite right for her job.

Stephanie has learned the secret of dressing for work. Your clothing should make you look good, not draw undue attention. We each have our own unique coloring, bone structure, and face shape. When you choose clothing that works with your individual characteristics, you look great. When you wear clothing that does not enhance your body structure or coloring, you appear sloppy or less attractive.

Well-designed clothes draw people's eyes to your face. This encourages eye-to-eye contact. Clothing that doesn't suit you will be distracting to others. They will notice your accessories, rather than your face. When you are well put-together, people remember that you look professional, rather than which individual items of clothing you were wearing.

Choose fabrics, colors and styles that emphasize your good features, and detract from your weaker features or figure flaws. What is appropriate for you won't suit someone else.

34. Why the colors you wear send a powerful message

Bonnie arrives at a meeting wearing pants and a bright orange shirt. Stephanie is wearing a charcoal gray pants suit with a white blouse. Which look do you think is most appropriate for a business meeting?

The colors you wear send a message. The image you project in a beige suit is quite different from the one you project when you wear navy. The darker the color, the more powerful you look. Monochromatic colors, such as different shades of gray, can make you look sophisticated. Bright colors make you look more informal.

Red is a powerful color that draws attention to you. It may work well if you are giving a speech, but not as well if you want to be seen as a team player. You will be taken more seriously in business if you avoid bright colors such as yellow or orange. Save these colors for casual situations.

In business you need colors like navy, gray and black as part of your wardrobe. If these colors don't suit you, add lighter or brighter colors near your face with a tie or scarf.

Tip Studies show that if you wear a navy blue suit or jacket to an interview you are more likely to get the job than if you wear any other color. There are many shades of navy. Choose the one that suits you best.

35. Why a "power ranger" watch makes you look like—a power ranger

Margaret is at a business meeting. She is wearing a smart-looking business suit, and good-quality leather shoes. When she checks the time, however, she reveals a plastic, multicolored watch. Tim is wearing a tailored suit, white shirt and elegant tie. His pulls a cheap plastic ballpoint pen out of his pocket to sign a contract.

The small details complete the picture. Everything you wear or carry in a business environment is part of your total image. A sports watch or inexpensive costume jewelry look out of place with your business suit. A plastic pen, or a worn-out shabby briefcase spoils the picture. You need to keep your look consistent.

Choose the best quality leather briefcase and accessories that you can afford. Choose gold, silver or leather accessories when possible. Invest in an elegant watch and a good-quality pen. Check your umbrella and luggage too. Are they in good repair, or coming apart at the seams? Although these items are functional, they still make a statement.

golden nugget 9 — The small details of your image complete the big picture.

36. Why clothes that whisper "safe and traditional" aren't always safe

Michael has an interview at an advertising agency, and he wants to look perfect. He wears a navy blue suit, crisp white shirt, and conservative tie. At his interview he notices that everyone in the office is dressed in casual, trendy clothes. Michael doesn't get the job.

Did you know that there is no such thing as neutral clothing? Everything you wear shows a decision you made. Your clothing is a non-verbal statement about who you are and what you do. If you wear inappropriate clothing to a job interview, people may question whether you know the industry well enough, and if you'll fit in with the company.

Don't assume that you need a conservative suit for every job. Ask people you know in similar jobs how they dress. Before you visit a company, check out the scene in the lobby of the building. Ask about the dress code when you are called for an interview, or call the Human Resources Department to ask. During the first crucial minutes of a job interview, when you are being judged, you may realize you're not dressed appropriately. You can say, "I'm not sure about the dress code here. I'm getting mixed signals. Is my look too traditional? (or too casual?)"

37. How to find the right level of formality for your job

Gail, a corporate lawyer, wants to project authority and competence. She wears suits to work. Like Gail, if you work with people in a conservative environment, you will probably wear the most formal clothes. In banking, insurance, and finance you need a traditional look to inspire trust.

Mark, in sales, meets the public every day. He generally wears a sports jacket and pants. If he visits a traditional company he wears a suit and tie. He tailors his look to his clients.

Tanya works in a government office. She usually wears an unmatched jacket and pants. Julie works at a database company. She wears business casual clothes, such as a turtleneck or polo shirt with pants. Her job is more technical, and she doesn't meet clients very often.

Think about your industry and how you want to be perceived. Look at the people above you and observe how they dress. If you want to be considered for promotion, you have to look the part to fit in.

golden nugget 10 Dress for the job you aspire to, not the job you have now.

Both men and women in the front lines dress for their clients. When we deal with TSE 300 companies, the suit and tie is still the uniform of the day. If the client is a high-tech IPO we might dress in business casual clothes. Support staff who work behind the scenes wear comfortable clothes such as khakis and flannel.

—Ian Blair, Bank of Montreal's Nesbitt Burns

You always make some kind of statement, powerful or inept, with the way you dress.

—**Robert Pante**

Your outer appearance is an expression of your inner control.

—**Anonymous**

Part 9

How to project "Champagne taste" on a "beer budget"

Everything should be made
as simple as possible,
and no simpler.
—Albert Einstein

38. A simple way to ensure that you are always well-dressed

How can you look and feel your best at all times? The secret lies in two small words: "Quality counts." If you buy the best quality clothes you can afford, you will feel great every time you wear them.

To find out if you are buying quality, look at the fabric. A suit that is 100% wool will wear better and last longer than a suit made of polyester, or a blend of materials. Cotton or silk shirts look and feel better than acrylic blends. Cheap fibers crease more easily and cling to your body. They will not have a smooth appearance. Good quality clothing is an investment. It is one you won't regret because the items will last longer, need less maintenance, and look better.

It's better to invest in one classic, good quality suit or jacket than several inexpensive outfits. When you wear clothing made from quality fiber you feel better. When you feel great in your clothes, you project confidence

39. The easiest way to always look well put-together

Take a quick count. How many accessories are you wearing? Accessories include eyeglasses, ornate belt buckles or shoe buckles, and scarves, as well as each individual piece of jewelry.

If you want to look well put-together, keep your business look simple. You will always look professional if you wear clean, classic lines and monochromatic colors. This works well even with casual clothes.

A common problem is over-accessorizing. If you wear multiples of anything, such as bracelets or rings, it may be "too much." Choose one piece of jewelry as a focal point. For women, an elegant pair of earrings or an unusual pin projects a more polished image than dangling earrings and numerous clanking bracelets. As for body piercing and tattoos, for both men and women, take your cues from those higher up in your organization.

40. Two key elements that reveal if you're "up-to-date"

John has oversized glasses and long sideburns—a look he adopted years ago. The trouble is, no one wears oversized glasses or sideburns any more. Helen's hairstyle was popular in high school, but she graduated from high school ten years ago.

Keep your look up-to-date. It shows that you are in touch with what's happening, and open to change. If you haven't changed with the times, it immediately shows your lack of awareness. It also makes you look old-fashioned. Styles, shapes and colors go in and out of vogue, and subtle changes make the difference between a current and a dated look.

Update your hairstyle and glasses when styles change. They are your most noticeable accessories, and you wear them every day. Find stores that cater to business professionals. Ask the sales people for advice on putting your wardrobe together. If you are "fashion-challenged," hire an image consultant. It's worth the investment. When you know you look your best, you'll exude confidence and poise.

golden nugget 11

You will always project a polished, professional image with a classic, up-to-date look.

Part 10

How to use clothing to project the appropriate level of authority

Clothes don't make the person, but they mark the person.
—Rose Marie Smith

41. How a formal look helps you show power and authority

Do you want to project power and authority? It's simple. Just follow these four rules.

1. You will project the most power and authority with a matched suit. It is more formal than a jacket with contrasting pants or a skirt.

2. Darker colors help you project a higher level of authority than lighter colors. A navy, charcoal or black suit is the most formal, especially when you wear it with a white or cream-colored shirt.

3. Smoother, plainer fabrics in solid colors give you a formal business look. The more bulky, textured or patterned your fabric, the more informal you look.

4. Keep your look simple. Wear a minimal number of prints or patterns on shirts and ties. The fewer details and colors you have, the more power you project.

42. How to appear more approachable by changing a few elements

If you work with the public, you want to look professional, yet approachable. What should you wear? You can create a friendly, welcoming look by changing one or two elements of your outfit. Here are some things to try, but don't do all of these things at once. You'll end up with a casual look.

1. Change the contrast: Wear your dark suit with a colored shirt or blouse.

2. Change the color: A lighter-colored gray or beige suit makes you look less formal than a dark blue suit.

3. Wear separates: A jacket with pants or a skirt of a different color is less formal than a matched suit.

4. Add texture or pattern: A tweed or patterned jacket is less formal than a solid-colored jacket. A print or floral tie or blouse softens the look of a dark suit.

5. Change the items (For women): Pants look less formal than a skirt. A dress is less formal than a suit. A collarless shirt looks less formal than a blouse.

43. How the power grid helps you go from traditional to trendy

Use this grid to help you fine-tune your business wardrobe.

	Item	Color	Contrast	Pattern/texture
MORE FORMAL	Matched suit	Dark: black, navy, charcoal	High contrast: dark suit with white or cream-colored shirt	Smooth, plain fabric
	Unmatched jacket & pants/skirt	Medium tones-gray, beige, taupe, blue	Less contrast: Different shades of the same color; Some texture or pattern	More texture: tweed, woven fabric More pattern: checks, floral, stripes, paisley
LESS FORMAL	Separates: Shirt/blouse Polo shirt Turtleneck Pants/skirt	Light colors Bright colors	Unmatched items	Bulky fabrics Shiny fabrics Knitted fabrics More details

44. How to look professional when you wear casual business clothes

Have you noticed that in some offices, business casual equals mass confusion? You may be overjoyed when your office institutes casual Fridays, or perhaps you wear casual clothes every day. But you, or others in your office, may not be sure what this means.

Scott Adams, the cartoonist who draws the business cartoon, *Dilbert*, writes, "I love the business casual look for the way it combines unattractive with unprofessional while diminishing neither."

Some staff members look as if they should be somewhere else—perhaps out jogging or curled up on the couch. Some clothes are just a bit too casual for work.

Remember that you want people to focus on your professional skills, not your body. If you wear anything that is extreme—very short, tight, low-cut or revealing, or looks like sportswear or beachwear, people may notice your clothes rather than your work.

45. Three levels of business casual help you tailor your look to your job

A good rule to remember is that business casual is a notch or two below what you would normally wear to work. Here are the three levels of business casual.

Level	1. Classic casual	2. Smart casual	3. Relaxed casual
Look	Approachable, open	Accessible, creative	Relaxed, friendly
Key items	Jacket	Jacket or sweater 2-3 piece outfits, Layers	Denim
Colors	Dark, bright	Any color	Any color
Shirts	With collar (tie not needed)	With collar/polo	With or without collar
Fabrics	Wool, linen, silk	Khaki, corduroy, knits	Flannel, denim, leather, suede
Women	Pantsuit	Sweater sets	Short sleeved, sleeveless blouses
Avoid	Short sleeves, sleeveless	Denim, shiny fabrics	Messages, slogans, shiny or sheer fabrics

I was conducting interviews to fill a position in our department, and a number of qualified candidates were called in. One candidate came to the interview stylishly dressed and displayed especially good manners as she shook hands with the interviewing team. She was offered the job.

One year later when I was leaving the department, I was asked to suggest a replacement for myself. The first person who came to mind was this same woman. Elizabeth's fast track to a higher position was directly linked to the outstanding first impression she had made one year before.

—Sandra Gruss, Consultant

46. Executives reveal the biggest "no-nos" on the job

Top executives in medium and large corporations were consulted about business casual clothing. The majority of them considered the following items unacceptable.

Athletic wear	Beach wear	Other styles
Jogging suits	Spandex	Short shorts
Tank tops without jackets	Tube tops without jackets	See-through tops
Sweat pants & sweat shirts	Halter tops without jackets	Bare midriffs
T-shirts with slogans	Plastic sandals or thongs	

Part 11

Why the small details count for so much

Never judge by appearances,
but remember—that's how
people will judge you.
—Anonymous

47. Why grooming is a basic component of your image

Do you work long hours? Do you travel a lot, and live out of a suitcase for days at a time? Sometimes it's hard to keep track of details such as getting clothes cleaned. And after a long hard day at the office we may not realize that we don't smell as fresh as we could. But other people notice.

If you ask a group of people what turns them off the most when they meet someone new, most people list dirty hair or fingernails, body odor, bad breath and stained clothing. It should go without saying that grooming is a key component of a powerful image.

Basic cleanliness includes daily bathing and deodorant, and clean clothes. These are essential for looking and feeling our best. Our hair, teeth and fingernails should always be clean and polished. If we use perfume or after-shave lotion, they should be used very lightly. We all want to make sure we look good and smell fresh at all times.

Tip It's a good idea to carry tissues with you. In a cold climate, your nose may run when you come inside. If you eat spicy food in a restaurant, a tissue can save the day. You never want to use a linen napkin to wipe your nose.

One of the most surprising and negative impressions I remember from my career in human resources was left by a thirty-five year old man. He was well qualified for a job in our research lab, and had a pleasant personality. But he arrived for his interview in jeans and run-down shoes, with his hair in a long scraggly ponytail.

The director explained that the job entailed some meetings with clients. The candidate cut him off with a grand gesture, and the astonishing words, "My look is non-negotiable, man. I'm a scientist."

I have often wondered what became of this man. He wasn't hired at our company.

—Elizabeth Hannesson, Business writer

48. How a quick-check in the mirror can show you off to your advantage

There's a saying, "Elephants don't bite. Mosquitoes do." Often it's the small things that cause the biggest problems. When we have threads hanging off a well-tailored suit, or buttons missing from a shirt, we take away from our professional image.

Here is a grooming checklist to use before leaving the house or during the day:

- ☐ Hair is clean, well styled, no dandruff
- ☐ Teeth are clean, no food stuck from lunch, breath is fresh
- ☐ Fingernails are clean, shaped, no chipped polish
- ☐ Makeup is well designed and applied
- ☐ No shaving cream left on face, no 5 o'clock shadow
- ☐ No loose buttons, hanging threads or hems
- ☐ No runs in stockings
- ☐ No underwear or slips showing
- ☐ Shoes are polished, not worn down at the heel

Tip Grooming repairs should be done in private, not in public. If you have to file a broken nail or pick spinach from your teeth, go to the nearest restroom.

49. Two places where your attention to detail always pays off

Have you noticed people who always look great? They always look up-to-date, without being over-the-edge. Chances are their hair looks terrific.

Your hair is your most important fashion accessory because it's the one thing you wear with every outfit. In fact, we often label people by their hair. How often do you hear someone called, "the redhead," or "the blonde"?

When you see someone with a great haircut, discretely ask for the name of the hairdresser. If the cost is more than you expect, think of it as cost-per-wear, and compare it to any other article of clothes. A good haircut also saves time every day. You don't have to struggle with hair that refuses to behave.

Your shoes may be the first and last item of clothing people notice about you. Think about it. When you leave a job interview, the last things the interviewer will see are the heels of your shoes. Make sure they aren't run down. Your shoes reveal your attention to detail. Select shoes that aren't unusual or inappropriate enough to draw attention to your feet. You want to keep attention on your face so that you can maintain eye contact.

There is no such thing as a minor detail. All details are major.

—Anonymous

Part 12

Why a business meal is much more than eating and drinking

If you had to choose between
Incredibly Advanced
Accounting for Overachievers
and Remedial Knife and Fork,
head for the silverware.
—Harvey Mackay

50. What your dining habits say about your character

About 50 percent of business today is conducted over food. The business lunch or dinner is more than a meal - it's an important way to build relationships with employers, clients and colleagues.

A business meal is often part of the interview process. While we eat together, we get to know potential clients or partners, make deals, and even decide futures. We also get together when people at the office are promoted or leave the job. At a business meal the boss you usually pass in the corridor gets to see you in action.

Think of everything that takes place during a business meal. We meet, sit down together, converse, order, eat and drink various kinds of foods and beverages, exchange business cards, and part company. If your dining companion grabs the breadbasket without offering it to you, or shovels food into his or her mouth, you may conclude that this person is aggressive or insensitive. You may wonder how this person will act if you do business together.

golden nugget 12 The reason for a business meal is building relationships. The setting is the restaurant.

51. Breakfast, lunch or dinner: what to expect

You may be invited to an early breakfast, a lunch at mid-day, or a leisurely dinner. Each meal has its own characteristics.

Meal	Time	Length of time	Discussion
Breakfast	Can begin as early as 6 or 7 a.m.	About 1 hour	Business talk begins when coffee arrives
Lunch	Can begin as early as 11 a.m.	1 ½–3 hours	Begins with small talk, host begins business talk, usually after ordering
Dinner	6 p.m. or later	Several hours	Small talk during dinner, business talk towards the end of the meal

52. How to have a great start to your business meal

You want your business meal to go smoothly. If you plan ahead, it will be a success from start to finish.

If you are the host, you should arrive at the restaurant ten minutes early, and wait for the guests at the entrance. If you are the guest you should be on time.

The maitre d' leads you to the table, with the guests preceding the host. The guest always gets the preferred seat, which may be the one facing towards the room, or the one facing a window with a scenic view. Enter your chair from the left, and exit from the right.

You can put a small purse on your lap, or on the floor under your chair. Make sure the straps are tucked away, so they don't trip the servers. Place a larger briefcase beside your chair. Put keys, gloves, or your cell phone in your pocket or purse, not on the table.

While you wait for other guests to arrive you can order drinks. Don't touch anything else at the table, however. Keep the table pristine until everyone has arrived. This shows that you have business class.

53. How to make your ordering smooth as butter

Have you ever had a business meal where everyone is doing something different? Some people have soup, others have salad, and someone else has nothing. What happens? You may end up eating while others watch you. It feels awkward.

Remember that the purpose of a business meal is to build business relationships. Eating actually comes second. Everyone at the table should order as a group. Then everyone eats the same number of courses and finishes at the same time.

- As a guest, don't order alcoholic beverages at a job interview. Some people fail to get jobs for this reason. Order a soft drink or sparkling water. As a host, keep in step with your guests. If they order alcoholic beverages, order a beverage as well. It doesn't have to be alcoholic.

- As a guest, don't order the most expensive items on the menu, or more than two courses, unless your host suggests you do so. Ordering something in the middle price range is usually a good idea.

- It's all right to ask about foods you are uncertain about, but don't badger the server about ingredients or cooking techniques.

54. Why the food you order may not look good on your shirt

Kim recently had a meal with some business associates. They went to a fancy French restaurant. The lights were dim, and the menu was difficult to decipher. Kim was not familiar with French food, so she decided to go along with what the server suggested. The food turned out to be bone marrow in a wine sauce. When Kim got home later, she noticed that her white blouse was splattered with red sauce. Fortunately, in the dim light of the restaurant it was unlikely anyone saw the red spots. Fortunately as well, they weren't there to see her red face afterwards.

Be careful what you order at a business meal. Order foods that are easy to eat with a knife and fork. Avoid foods that are sticky or greasy, or foods you eat with your fingers. Save difficult dishes such as lobster, French onion soup, or pastas with sauces for when you eat with friends and family. At a business meal, stick with easy-to-eat, familiar foods. That way you don't end up wearing your food!

55. Basic table manners your mother probably taught you

Business dining may be new to you, but basic table manners are no surprise. They are based on the rules we learned at the table as we grew up. Remember this simple rule: any behavior that is unappetizing is considered discourteous. Here are some reminders.

1. Sit up straight. Don't slouch at the table, tip back on your chair, or circle your plate with your arms.

2. Chew with your mouth closed. Take small bites, chew and swallow before speaking.

3. Don't wave your utensils or play with your food.

4. Don't leave your knife and fork handles hanging off your plate. When you're not using your knife and fork, keep them on the plate.

5. Eat bread in bite-size pieces. Don't butter the whole piece of bread and bite into it.

6. Use your napkin to dab your mouth and fingers.

56. Your table setting is a roadmap for the meal

Here are a few simple rules for navigating the table setting.

- Use the utensils nearest the hand that holds it—forks on the left, knives and spoons on the right.
- The number of any utensil shows the number of courses. There is a maximum of three of any utensil at a time. Three forks indicate there will be a salad, main course and dessert, for example.
- Glasses are to the right because most people are right-handed. Remember: “drink” and “right” are both 5-letter words.
- Plates for bread or salad are to your left. Remember: “food” and “left” are both 4-letter words.
- Always start with the utensils on the outside and work towards the center.
- A desert spoon and fork may be above the dinner plate, or may be brought later.

57. Sweet endings that show you have business class

You want your business meal to end on the right note. If you are the host, you will want to escort your guests to the door, shake their hands and thank them for coming. You may want to discuss a follow-up to the meal. For example, you may say you'll call them in a few days to set up the next meeting.

As the guest, be sure to thank the host or hostess in person. You should also send a thank-you note. A hand-written note is best, but if your writing is illegible, you can type the note. Try to send it within 48 hours.

Don't pass out your business card during a meal. The time to exchange cards is at the end of the meal, before you part company.

The world was my oyster, but I used the wrong fork.

—Oscar Wilde

Part 13

How to shine at business events

Etiquette is the noise not
made while eating soup.
—Anonymous

58. How to have better buffet behavior

Sarah, a corporate executive, noted that she would never hire a particular firm as financial advisers after she saw them attack a buffet table, elbowing each other out of the way. For some reason, many people act as if the buffet is their last meal.

It's easy to avoid "animal behavior" if you take a moment to observe the set up. Are there two lines, with utensils and plates at either end? Join the smaller line. The food is the same.

Don't heap your plate with food. It's okay to start with soup or salad, then return for the main course. If you notice that a particular dish is in short supply, take a small serving. Use the serving spoon or fork that is intended for each dish.

Tip No "double-dipping." After you've put dressing on your carrot stick, or dipped your potato chip and bitten into it, don't return it to the bowl for more. Put some sauce or dip onto your plate, and dip from there.

59. How to juggle food and drinks while shaking hands

Have you ever had this experience at a cocktail party? You have a cold drink in your hand. You reach out to shake someone's hand, and say something like, "Sorry about my cold, wet hand." An apology isn't the best way to start a relationship.

It isn't easy to balance a drink and food, while eating and making small talk. Yet it's what we do at business cocktail parties or receptions. Here's a trick you can use. It's called "layering."

Hold everything in your left hand to leave your right hand clean and dry, ready to shake hands. To do this, hold your plate in your left hand. Put your glass on the plate, and anchor it with your thumb. A wine glass works well, but you can do this with a regular glass as well. Hold your napkin under the plate. Wipe your fingers after picking up your cold, wet drink.

Choose hors d'oeuvres and finger foods that are easy to eat. Use your right hand to pick up the small bits of food from your plate. Eat, and wipe your fingers on your napkin right afterwards. Voila! You're ready to shake hands at any time!

60. How to use party tricks to make you look savvy

Here are a few tricks to make you look party savvy at any business event.

Beer drinkers: Use a glass at a cocktail party. You can drink from a bottle when you're at home, or at your local pub. It goes without saying: drink responsibly. A business function is not the place to get loaded.

Cocktail eaters: Stay with easy-to-eat food. Be careful of sauces that drip, or foods that make your fingers sticky or greasy.

Toothpick hazards: Never put a used toothpick on a serving tray. If you can't find a nearby receptacle, put used toothpicks in an ashtray, or on your napkin.

Hot stuff: Be careful of hors d'oeuvres that may have extremely hot interiors. Take a small bite first to check the temperature and avoid burning your mouth. Also watch out for puff pastries that break open and splash innocent bystanders. Your potential boss or client won't appreciate having the contents of your snack on his or her suit jacket.

Part 14

How networking can help you reach your goals

Networking is people connecting
with people, linking ideas
and resources.
—Jessica Lipnack and
Jeffrey Stamps,
The Networking Book

61. How to change "networking terror" to "networking triumph"

Do you break into a cold sweat when you receive an invitation to a business cocktail party? Does the thought of a networking event strike terror in your heart? Walking into a room full of strangers is never easy. Studies show that over 40 percent of adults feel nervous about meeting new people. One survey showed that about 75 percent of people feel uncomfortable at business and social events. Perhaps this is because our parents always told us not to talk to strangers when we were young.

It's important to gain skills in networking, however, because networking gives you opportunities to meet prospective employers, clients and people who can influence your career.

It's also important to know that you don't have to be a born networker. It is easier for some people to approach new people than for others, but everyone can acquire these skills. To begin, review parts three and four of this book that deal with introductions.

golden nugget 13 Networking connects you with people who can help you reach your business goals.

62. How to get big benefits from networking

What are your business goals? Whatever they are, networking may be the most efficient way to reach them. Mark Granovetter, a researcher, studied hundreds of professional and technical workers. He found that:

- 56 percent found jobs through acquaintances
- 18 percent found jobs through newspaper ads or headhunters
- 20 percent got jobs by applying directly to companies

When you meet someone new, you don't connect with only one new person—you have the opportunity to connect with this person's sphere of contacts. You increase your chances of getting the job or clients you want when you are referred by a common acquaintance. If you want to meet a specific individual, you can usually find someone who knows that person—just by asking four or five people.

Your goal at a networking event is to make contacts—not to make sales. Networking is for gathering information. When you connect with someone who has business potential for you, arrange to meet at one of your offices, or at lunch or dinner. Networking connects you with people who can help you reach your business goals.

In the new economy, networking for yourself is an on-going career management activity, not just something you do between jobs. Networking is a skill. Like any skill, it takes practice to be good at it. So get practicing!

—Douglas Cameron,
Ontario Regional Director, Exec-U-Net Canada

It's always a big person who walks up to you and offers his/her hand and says hello.

—David J. Schwartz, *The Magic of Big Thinking*

63. How to prepare so your networking event will be a success

You'll be more successful at a networking event if you define your objectives before you go. For example, you may want to meet someone in the printing business, a new supplier for your company, or five new potential clients.

Before the function, find out who will be present and get information about them. Your knowledge will impress them.

Plan your wardrobe and accessories in advance. Think about adding an eye-catching accessory, such as an unusual tie, watch, or pin, as a conversation starter.

Plan to spend five to ten minutes with each person you meet. When you find someone you want to know better, set up a meeting. Then move on to talk to someone new.

Tip If the event is after work and you are ravenous, eat something before you arrive. If this is impossible, sit down and eat for a few minutes when you arrive, then get up and circulate. Don't try to talk to people while you're filling up. Remember, the purpose of networking is to make contacts. That's why it's called "network," not "net-sit" or "net-eat."

If you look warm and welcoming in person, you'll usually appear that way on television. Be confident, but not cocky. A smile and a sense of humor are important.

**—Sean O'Shea, Business Anchor and Editor,
Global Television Network, Toronto**

Part 15

Getting the most out of networking events

The best part about
networking is that everyone
wins because everyone helps
everyone else.
—Jan F. Triplett

64. Why it's easy to remember names at a networking event

What's the most difficult and important thing about meeting a new person? Remembering the person's name. The good news about a networking event is that people wear nametags. That makes your job a lot easier.

Here's a trick. Put your nametag on your right shoulder where people can read it easily. When you shake hands, your eyes naturally rest on the other person's right shoulder. Don't hide your nametag on a lower pocket, or on your handbag. Also, be careful about hanging your nametag near your waist on a string. You don't want people scanning your chest for your tag!

Tip: You can use your business card as your nametag. If your name is too small, write it in a larger size and attach it to your nametag. Another idea is to put your company name or your job title on your nametag. This helps people remember what you do, and it's a conversation-starter.

65. How to connect with people when you feel all alone

How do you feel before a networking event? If approaching strangers makes you feel apprehensive, here are a few tips to make it easier.

1. Position yourself near the door. That way you get to talk to a lot of people for a short amount of time.

2. The best person to approach is someone standing alone. He or she is probably feeling awkward, and will be grateful to be rescued when you approach.

3. Know that people always congregate at the bar or food table. Approach, and make comments to whoever is there about the food, the decor, and the event.

4. Remember the old saying, "two's company, three's a crowd"? Two people who are deep in conversation may not want to be interrupted. Look for groups of three or more people to approach.

5. Assume the role of host. Introduce others that you know. Offer to show people where the telephone or restroom is, if they ask. Soon you'll be chatting like old friends.

66. How to establish instant rapport with strangers

The best secret for shy people is that most people are worried themselves about being rejected. They're not judging you. We've all been rejected at one time or another, and the feeling remains for a long time. In business situations, however, most people are interested in connecting with others. That's why they go to networking events. In fact, many people want to meet new people, but end up talking with their colleagues because they are shy about approaching strangers.

To increase your chances of success, take a moment to study the body language of different groups in the room. Find a group where the people look like they are enjoying themselves and are having a light-hearted conversation, rather than two people who are talking intently. Approach the group and listen to the conversation for a few moments. When there is a pause, introduce yourself.

Say something like, "Hi, I'm Joan. I don't know anyone here, so I thought I'd introduce myself." Most people have been in your shoes, and will empathize. Ask about the function, why other people are there, or if they have been there before. If you don't know what to say, you can simply ask, "How's business?"

Remember to be sincere, smile, make eye contact and show interest by listening. Expect acceptance and you will be accepted.

67. How a "USP" makes a memorable introduction

Ted: "So what do you do?"
Allison: "I'm an accountant. What do you do?"
Ted: I'm a systems analyst."
Allison: "Oh. That's interesting....."

How often have you heard a business conversation like this? When you meet someone new, you have 60 seconds to capture his or her interest. A "USP," or "unique selling proposition" works wonders. When you say, "I'm a financial analyst," it says who you are, not what you do. It's important to tell people what you do, how you can benefit them, and what is special about your services. A financial analyst might say, "I help people keep their hard-earned money in their pockets." Here are more examples:

"Hello, my name is Ian Thomas. I can help you keep the world in focus. I'm an optician."

"Hi, I'm Jenny Blaire. I help people find the right location for their business. I'm the Ace of Space!"

Prepare and practice your USP so it will come out naturally. Imagine that you meet someone interesting in an elevator. Your USP will help you connect within seconds.

golden nugget 14 Make a memorable introduction within 60 seconds using a USP.

68. How to work the room like a master networker

Have you ever noticed a "master networker"? This person knows exactly what to do. He or she seems to enter and exit from groups gracefully, and to talk to almost everyone present. You can increase your effectiveness by using their techniques.

1. Circulate and meet different people. Don't sit down. It puts you out of the game.

2. Spend five or ten minutes with each person. Then approach another group or individual.

3. Prepare some conversation topics. See the section on "small talk" for ideas.

4. Have your business cards handy. Offer your card to people you would like to contact in the future.

People who have made a great first impression on me are the ones who have a positive outlook, and an up-lifting feeling about them. They pay attention to the details of how they present themselves physically, and the manner in which they speak with you. They are respectful listeners, interested not only in themselves but in what others have to say as well.

—Sandra Roscanu, Senior Marketing Manager, Pearson Education

Your best source of learning is the people you meet, so what are you waiting for?

—Michel Daigle, Communic.aide

69. Why you need your business cards at your fingertips

Has this ever happened to you? You reach into your pocket and hand someone your business card. They look at it, and look back at you with a puzzled expression. Then they say something like, "I didn't know you worked at the Handy Dandy Hardware Store." What happened? You've handed them someone else's business card.

Before a networking event, organize the things you need. Put your business cards in a pocket or a place where you can access them easily. Put the cards you receive in another pocket. That way you don't mix them up. Keep a pen handy in case you want to write down important information.

A good way to end a conversation is by exchanging business cards. When you offer your business card, it is a signal for closing your discussion and moving on to another group.

Tip A business card has value, and it's disrespectful to write on someone's card when they hand it to you. You can write information on it after you part company. If you need to take down some information immediately, ask the person's permission to write on his or her card.

70. How to exit a conversation with grace and style

You know the routine. You finally get a conversation going, and neither of you knows how to end the conversation graciously. So you end up talking with only one person, and don't make other contacts.

A good way to finish a conversation is to exit immediately after you have spoken, rather than after the other person has spoken. You don't want to appear rude by breaking off after someone has been talking to you.

Be careful of making excuses such as, "I'm going to get something to eat," or, "I'm going to the bar." The other person may decide to accompany you to the food table, or ask you to bring him or her a drink. Even announcing you are going to the restroom can be risky. People have been known to accompany others there (hopefully of the same gender!).

One exit that usually works is, "I'm going to make a phone call." People seldom accompany you to the telephone. But the best way to exit a conversation is simply to say, "It's been great talking to you," shake hands and move on. There's no need for explanations.

71. How to keep networking after the event is over

Have you gone to networking events and wondered why you never got any new business? Going to a networking meeting without following up is only half the job.

Right after you meet someone new, write down important information about them. You can write personal information as well. This will give you a reason to connect later. If you learn, for example, that a potential client is looking for a dog-training school for his new pooch, you can call with information you have in this area.

Follow up your valuable leads with calls or letters. A personal, handwritten note is best, but you can also type a letter on your letterhead. Arrange to meet at one of your offices, or for coffee or lunch.

Finally, deliver what you promise. Send the brochure, article or information you discussed.

Part 16

Small talk is anything but small

Too often we lose an
opportunity to meet someone
because we spend precious
time trying to think of the
perfect opening line.
—Susan RoAne
How to Work a Room

72. Small talk isn't a skill you're born with—it's a skill you can learn

John approaches Susan at a networking event. He introduces himself, and asks, "So, are you from around here?" Susan answers, "No." John searches desperately for something to say. "Do you know anyone at this event?" Susan replies, "Not really. How about you?" "Me neither," John answers.

After a few minutes of uncomfortable silence, John says, "Well, nice to meet you." "Yeah, you too," Susan says. They part company. Each of them is thinking, "Boy, it sure is hard to connect with anyone."

We all know that small talk is an important skill. What we may not know is that it's a skill that can be acquired. How much better if Susan had volunteered where she came from, or if John had asked Susan about her background? Techniques for better small talk are easy to learn, and the rewards are great.

golden nugget 15 Small talk is important because it leads to big talk.

73. How to use opening lines to break the ice

Do you have an opening line? Actually, almost anything will do. Just remember to keep it positive. After all, no one wants to start a conversation with someone who is complaining about the food, the music or the ambiance.

A compliment is always a welcome opener. Comment on the person's unusual tie or pin, or on the delicious hors d'oeuvres. Any topic in the news is also a good icebreaker. Come prepared with some ideas.

Clichés, or "golden oldies" are fine as conversation starters. After all, that's why we use them. Talking about the weather is a standard opening because it works. Everyone has something to contribute about the latest heat wave, ice storm, or glorious spring day.

74. How to pick up on what people say to spark a conversation

Terri and Mike have just met. Mike mentions that he just got back from Vancouver. Terry can answer in one of these ways:

"I just love Vancouver. It's such a beautiful city. What was the highlight of your trip?"

"I've never been to Vancouver, but I'm hoping to go some day. What would you recommend to a tourist?"

Either way, Terri asks open-ended questions that invite conversation. Use questions that open up the conversation. They begin with: who, what, where, when, why and how. Avoid "yes/no" questions that can be answered in monosyllables.

Be careful about conversation stoppers such as, "We already tried that. It didn't work." Instead, ask questions and use verbal prompts to encourage conversation. You can say, "Please tell me more about...," "What other aspects have you considered...," or just, "How interesting..." Also, remember that a sincere compliment, and a smile or laugh in the appropriate place, will make others want to converse with you.

75. How to be a great conversationalist while saying very little

"She's a great conversationalist," is often said about a person who doesn't talk very much. How is this possible? It's because she does something even more important - she listens. People who listen actively turn their full attention to the speaker. This is difficult to do, because most people are busy thinking of what to say next, rather than fully concentrating on what the speaker is saying.

Use body language and "filler" words to show that you're listening. Lean towards the person slightly when they are speaking. Nod your head, and use filler words such as, "uh huhh," "yes," or "I see."

Make eye contact. If you find it too intense to look into the speaker's eyes, look at any part of the face, from hairline to chin. Break eye contact momentarily when you are speaking, then return your gaze to the speaker.

One of the most powerful ways of developing rapport is to demonstrate your interest in another. Many of us think we listen well, but what we think is not the issue. We are not the significant judges of our listening competence. The speaker is the real judge.

Ask your partner (professional or personal) how often they feel you are not listening. Ask them what you do that makes them feel like you are not listening. Then ask them what you do that demonstrates to them that you are listening. You now know what to do. One of the most effective ways is by restating what you just heard.

—Tom Stoyan, Canada's Sales Coach

Did you know? The Chinese character for listening is composed of the ears, the eyes and the heart.

76. How to use the "echo" technique to keep the conversation going

To keep a conversation going, try to pick up on the last thing the other person says. Here's how it works.

Susan: "I'm expanding my printing business."

John: "Your printing business...?

Susan: "Yes, I want to give my customers a fuller range of services. You know, like quick copying, color copying..."

John: "Quick copying and color copying...?"

Susan: "Yes, customers seem to need these services...

And so the conversation goes. For a change of pace, so you don't sound like an echo, use "extenders" such as, "Uh huhhh..., tell me more..., interesting..." It's amazing how long you can keep a conversation going in this way.

77. How to prepare for small talk by knowing "what's up"

Small talk is anything but "small." Being a good conversationalist is crucial to making connections. To get ready for small talk:

- Be up on current events. Read at least one newspaper every day.
- Clip and save articles of interest from newspapers and magazines.
- Read professional journals and newsletters in your field to keep up-to-date.
- Be knowledgeable about concerts, sports events and movies that have just opened in your city or community.
- Use a funny story from the newspaper, or a personal anecdote to start a conversation. Humor brings people together.

78. How to avoid putting a "downer" on the conversation

Are you interested in hearing about plane crashes? How about the number of people in the office with the flu?

Topics that upset everyone, such as grim statistics about disasters, put a "downer" on the conversation. Personal topics such as health problems or a recent operation may also be a turn-off. Sure, there are lots of problems in the world. But people don't want to be reminded of them at a business event. They want to loosen up a bit, and enjoy themselves.

Controversial topics such as religion and politics often stir up heated arguments, and are sometimes difficult to avoid. If you find yourself in the midst of an emotional discussion you can simply say, "Some people see it that way. Another way to look at it is...," or, "I tend to side with people who say..." Be careful not to directly criticize another person's opinion, however.

Jokes can be a great way to connect with people, but first, think about whom they might offend. Avoid any jokes that are racial, cultural or sexual. They are big turn-offs for more people than you can imagine. Be especially careful about jokes about people. You never know who is the sister-in-law, or the second cousin, of whom.

79. Why a conversation is like a tennis game

Have you met the "conversation hog"? The conversation hog always wants to be in the spotlight. He or she always has a story to top yours, and can't wait to tell it. In fact, you can forget about telling your story. The conversation hog doesn't want to hear it.

A conversation is like a tennis game. You start the conversation and then send the ball into the other court. The other person continues the conversation and then sends it back to you. Without this give and take, you end up with a monologue. It gets boring and tiresome. Then the other person wants "out."

Be upbeat and enthusiastic, and contribute to the conversation. Respond with interest and energy to what people say, and give positive reinforcement. Your enthusiasm will make people appreciate you as a conversationalist because they will feel you are interested in what they have to say. You will always be a welcome conversation partner.

80. The biggest irritant in a conversation, and what to do about it

What irritates you most in a conversation? Chances are it is being continually interrupted. It's annoying when you can't finish your thoughts.

Surveys show that being interrupted is the number one turn-off for most people. You may even be guilty of this without being aware of it. If people frequently say to you, "Please let me finish," you may be interrupting others more than you realize.

Focus on what the speaker is saying, rather than on your next comment. Then you will have an easier time letting the speaker finish his or her thoughts. Just because someone pauses briefly, it doesn't mean they have finished speaking. Give them time to complete their thoughts. Then they'll be more likely to want to hear yours.

Paradoxically, to make a great first impression you have to stop focusing on yourself and start focusing on the other person. Relationship building is vital in business today. Your ability to connect positively with others is a critical skill.

—Diane Bussandri,
BUSSANDRI MACDONALD CONSULTING GROUP

Over the years I've had the good fortune to meet many business leaders, professionals, and plain ordinary folks who left lasting impressions. The key quality shared by all was the ability to "talk slowly and listen quickly"— they preferred to learn about me rather than talk about themselves.

—Mark Berkowitz, Executive Director, Exec-U-Net Canada

Part 17

Your only chance to make a first impression may be on the phone

A good beginning
makes a good ending.
—English proverb

81. Why a telephone call is your verbal handshake

At least 75 percent of the business we conduct begins with a phone call. In some cases it's the only contact you have with a person. The way you sound on the telephone is the first, and sometimes the only, impression you make.

We use phone calls to introduce ourselves, give and get information, set up appointments, and follow up on previous contacts. The initial phone call can influence whether you get the job interview, the new client or the meeting you want.

On the telephone, the person you are speaking with cannot see how you are dressed, your body language, or your office. The only criteria for pursuing the business relationship are the words you use, and the way you use your voice. Peoples' conclusions about your ability and trustworthiness are based on your voice and telephone manner.

golden nugget 16

Your first impression on the telephone may be the only one you get to make.

On the telephone, you don't have your physical attributes to help you make a great first impression. You may be well dressed and impeccably groomed, but no one can see you. If you sound insecure, you won't come across well. When you call someone, you have to be prepared to adjust to the person's tone and mood within five seconds. Listen carefully to how they speak, and take it from there.

—Mireille Tanguay,
Manager, Customer Relations and Personal Shopping,
Birks

82. Two tricks to give your voice warmth and energy

Do people often ask you to repeat what you just said? Perhaps you are mumbling or not enunciating clearly. Often a friend can give you feedback on the effect of your voice. A good telephone voice is clear and loud enough for people to hear, without yelling or sounding shrill.

When your voice sounds pleasant, people want to listen to you. People with high-pitched voices are often perceived of as unprofessional. Voice tones that are nasal, raspy or thin are also unattractive.

Energy is important to the quality of your voice. A good trick to remember is that when you are sitting during a phone call, your diaphragm is compressed. When you stand up and move around, you breath more freely. You have more energy, which will come across in your voice.

Another trick is to smile when you speak. The person you speak to won't see the smile, but the warmth that comes from a smile will come across the phone line!

83. Three keys to successful phone calls

Before you make an important call, take a few moments to prepare. You'll increase your chances of getting what you want.

1. Know the reason for your call, and prepare any information or questions you need. It helps to write notes on a paper, so you don't get sidetracked during the conversation.

2. Have all the materials you need at hand. This includes a pen and paper, your calendar for setting appointments, and other information you have from previous contacts. This way you don't have to put someone on hold to search for the facts or figures you need.

3. Take notes. During the call, write down the relevant points you discussed. This shows your efficiency and attention to detail, and helps avoid repeat phone calls for the same information.

84. How to make your phone calls sound professional

When you make a business call, begin with “Hello” rather than “Hi!” which sounds unprofessional. Leave a brief pause, and then identify yourself. Say your first and last name. If you are calling for your company, say the name of your company and department.

“Hello. This is Jane Smith from XYZ Company, calling for Bob Jones.”

“This is John Brown, ABC Company, accounting department, returning Susan Green’s call.”

When the receptionist has to ask who you are, you sound inexperienced in business. Convey your professionalism by giving your name and company affiliation immediately.

85. Four tips for making a great impression when you answer the phone

1. Answer the phone as promptly as you can—within three rings, if possible. This shows people that their calls are important to you.

2. Greet the caller by saying "Hello," "Good morning," or "Good afternoon." Give your name and your department or company.

3. Speak clearly and courteously, with a smile in your voice. Use the caller's name whenever possible. Write down important information.

4. End the call on a positive note, and use the caller's name. You can say, "It's been a pleasure talking to you, Ms. Smith." Don't be too quick to put the receiver back. Hearing a phone bang in your ear isn't pleasant. The other person may think you hung up on them!

86. How bad telephone messages can leave you scratching your head

Imagine receiving a message like this: "This is Rita Menxlxlxlx. Please call me at 613- 835-mbmbm." What makes this message difficult to get?

1. The last name is mumbled and said too quickly. You know your own name, but other people don't. It's important to say your name clearly and slowly. If your name is unusual or difficult to pronounce, spell it.

2. The phone number is said too quickly. People can't write down your name and 10 digits if you say them at break-neck speed. This is all new information to them.

3. The information is only given once. If the person you are calling doesn't know you, repeat your name at the end of the message. Repeat your telephone number. The receiver will be grateful not to have to re-listen to your message several times to get the information.

Most people tell me they expect to get voice mail when they place a business call. If that is the case, then why do they sound like they are surprised when they leave a message? They lose an opportunity to leave a clear, concise and powerful message.

Prior to placing your call, consider writing out your message, at least in point form. Then ask yourself what primary impression you want to leave. Warm and friendly? Powerful? Clear and to-the-point? Reflective? Considerate? Understanding?

Voice mail is a powerful tool in the hands of professionals. They decide how they want to be thought of, and then invest the time to perform accordingly.

Others don't get an impression of you. You give them an impression. Each time you pick up the phone, you get to decide what impression you want to leave.

—Tom Stoyan, Canada's Sales Coach

87. Why you, not your dog, should be on your voice message

Have you ever called someone and heard the family dog barking a message? How about a child's voice saying, "We aren't home now. Please call back." This may be all right for messages between close friends, but if a company calls you for a job interview, you won't come across as being very impressive.

If you are in the business world, you need a professional message that is clear and concise. Don't use cute sound effects or gimmicks. Don't use children's voices, or the sound of your dog barking. Stay away from jokes or catchy tunes. What sounds cute to you is annoying to others. What may be funny the first time isn't funny if someone calls more than once and hears the same tired joke.

Here is a basic format for a professional message. It's a good idea to write your message and practice it a few times so it sounds smooth.

"This is Jason Black. Please leave your name and number and I'll get back to you shortly."

88. How to sound sophisticated by slashing your telephone slang

What image do you get when you hear this message: "I can't come to the phone because I'm tied up right now."? Do you wonder what exactly this person is doing? It sounds a bit kinky, doesn't it? Instead, try: "I'm not available at the moment. Please leave a message and I'll return your call."

Too much casual speech in a business setting can cause you problems. Remember—the other person can't see you, so your language is more important than ever. Watch out for phrases such as, "Hang on a moment." What should the caller hang on to? If you have to put someone on hold, always ask permission first. You can say, "May I put you on hold for a moment, or would you prefer that I call you back?"

Think about how you end the conversation. "Bye-bye" sounds like what your mother taught you when you waved to someone. "Good-bye" makes you sound sophisticated.

89. How to avoid the biggest telephone offence

How do you feel when you are in someone's office, and they answer the phone and have a long conversation? Irritated and annoyed? You're not alone.

The person you are with is always more important than someone calling on the telephone. The most common offence people commit is forgetting this. If someone calls you during a business appointment, let your answering machine take a message. If you are expecting a very important call, apologize to the person you are with, answer the phone and set an appointment to call back.

Similarly, when you are on the phone and you hear a beep from another call, let the phone ring. Your answering service will take the message. If you are speaking to someone you know well, you can ask if they mind waiting momentarily while you check who is calling. Remember that the person you are with takes precedence. Arrange to call the other person back as soon as possible.

90. Dos and don'ts to maximize your effectiveness

A few simple tips can help you maximize your phone effectiveness.

Do If you are calling from home, make your calls away from distracting noises such as the washing machine or TV.

Do Stick to your point and keep it brief. Business people don't have time for chatty conversations during the day. Be careful not to get sidetracked. It gives the impression that time is not important for you.

Don't Eat, chew gum or drink during a business conversation. No one likes to hear a chewing sound in his or her ear. Avoid rustling papers or working at your computer. The other person will realize you are not giving him or her your full attention.

Courtesy costs nothing but reaps rich rewards.

—Anonymous

Part 18

Business correspondence—first impressions by mail

Words are, of course,
the most powerful drug
used by mankind.
—Rudyard Kipling

91. Why your business letter creates a powerful first impression

Black type on paper has power. The first impression you make may not be in person or on the telephone. It may be in a business letter.

Your business letter is more than just a message—it has substance. Business letters are permanent records that show you off to your best or worst advantage. People keep letters. They may take them out and refer to them later. Letters may be passed on to other people. People who have already met you will form a new opinion of you the first time they read your letter.

You make a powerful first impression with a concise, clear letter. A poorly formatted letter, full of typos and spelling errors makes you look weak and unprofessional. Make sure your letter creates and reinforces a powerful first impression.

golden nugget 17

Use your business correspondence to make a permanent, professional impression.

92. Why a sharp-looking document makes you look sharp

Have you received any letters that are so confusing you don't know what to read first? Chances are the writer used too many typefaces. Modern computers give us dozens of typefaces. This doesn't mean you have to use them all! Choose two typefaces—one for display, or headlines, and the other for the body of the text.

Use consistent formatting. Choose either block style (everything is flush left) or semi-block (indenting each paragraph, with the date and closing salutation on the right). Block style is most popular today. (See the appendix for sample letter forms.)

Keep your letter concise. Experts in business correspondence say that your paragraphs should be no more than seven lines long. And don't cram too much onto one page. The body of the letter should be two to three paragraphs long. If your letter is longer, use a second page.

93. How to structure your letter to show you mean business

Sylvia, a human resources manager, frequently gets letters addressed "Ladies and Gentlemen," or "To whom it may concern." These letters generally end up in the garbage. Sylvia says, "I'm a busy person. When someone can't be bothered to find out the name of the person they are writing to, I can't be bothered to read their letter."

Start off your letter with the salutation. Use the first name if you know the person well. Use the honorific (Mr. or Ms) and last name for someone you don't know.

The body of your letter conveys information. Begin the first paragraph by stating the purpose of your letter. Be concise and clear. End with a request for action.

An appropriate close is "Sincerely," for a formal letter, or "Regards," for a less formal letter.

94. Five secrets to getting what you want from your business letters

A business letter has a purpose. It is either to give information, or to request action. Here are five ways to accomplish your goal.

1. Begin with a clear statement of why you are writing and what you expect.

2. Remember whom you are writing to so that your tone is appropriate.

3. Give the information your reader needs in order to carry out your request.

4. Keep the letter simple and factual. Avoid unnecessary or personal information.

5. End with a suggested action, either one you will take, or one you want the reader to take.

95. Why a hand-written note sets you above the crowd

Don't you feel special when you receive a hand-written note in the mail? It's usually the piece of mail you read first when it arrives with a pile of bills or advertisements.

We all want to be appreciated and acknowledged. When you send a hand-written word of thanks or congratulations, it sets you above the crowd. This is because not many people take the time to write notes.

How do you know when to write a thank-you note? That's simple. Any time someone takes more than 15 minutes to do you a favor or help you, write a note. A thank-you note shows that you:

1. Acknowledge and appreciate it when someone does something for you

2. Are a professional who follows through

3. Are a person who goes the extra mile

96. The easiest way to write a personal note

A thank-you note doesn't have to be long. Three sentences are fine, as in the example below. Here's how to do it.

1. Begin with an expression of thanks for the event or favor.

2. Add a sentence about how it affected you, or how much you appreciated the kindness.

3. Conclude with best wishes or a statement about a future meeting.

Dear Bob,

It was a pleasure meeting you at the networking event on Wednesday. I enjoyed discussing the job market with you, and appreciate your tips about job leads. I look forward to seeing you at the meeting next month.

Sincerely,

Dan

The handwritten note…reflects personal care, thought, and time expended.

—Susan RoAne
Keynote speaker/ best-selling author
How to Work a Room

Part 19

Techno-etiquette: communication in the electronic age

Never let a computer know
you're in a hurry.
—Anonymous

97. How to use a cell phone without annoying people around you

Jack is at a business lunch when his cell phone rings in his briefcase. Diners at other tables look over in annoyance. His colleagues stop their conversation while he tries to cover the phone and speak privately. Susan takes out her phone and carries on a loud conversation about a new contract as she waits in the dentist's office. Other patients glare in her direction.

Using a cell phone around others shows a lack of consideration, and makes you look indiscrete and unprofessional. If you have to use a cell phone in public, try to find a private spot, and keep the call brief. Be careful about who you call on a cell phone. The recipient has to pay, and may not appreciate a call that could wait for another time.

Turn off cell phones in any enclosed public space such as an elevator, plane, train, or restaurant. Avoid using them in waiting rooms, meetings, theatres or other places where you can disturb others. And be careful about using a cell phone when driving. It's distracting, and can cause an accident. Pull over if you must make a call.

98. How to make your fax correspondence flawless

When you send a fax in a business context, you need to be as attentive as you are with other correspondence. Always include a cover sheet that shows the following:

- The sender's and recipient's names
- The sender's and recipient's fax number
- The sender's telephone number
- The date
- The number of pages sent

Use a subject line to let the recipient know the reason for the fax. If you are sending a fax that is more than five pages, let the recipient know. In that case you may want to include a brief message about the material you are sending.

To avoid difficult-to-read faxes, be sure to leave ample margins. Small characters may be hard to read in a fax. To improve visibility you can use 14 or 16 points. It's a good idea to call after sending a fax to make sure it was received in good order, with no pages missing.

99. Why your e-mail may be fast but it shouldn't be sloppy

With the click of a mouse we can reach people across town or around the world instantly. But with our ability to communicate so quickly, we sometimes sacrifice accuracy for efficiency. We can also become sloppy, or even offend others, without realizing it. Just because e-mail is fast doesn't mean that anything goes.

When you write an e-mail message, apply the same rules you use when writing a business letter. Use correct grammar, spelling and terms of address. Be clear and concise in your communications.

Include a subject line that states the reason for your communication. People in business may receive hundreds of messages. They don't have time to wonder what a message is about when they sort their mail. Make sure your messages are clear so people will have an easy time responding to them.

100. E-mail do's and don'ts to be techno-savvy

With billions of messages sent every day, we have a new set of guidelines for courteous e-mail behavior. It's called "netiquette." Here are a few basic rules.

Do use e-mail for a reasonably short message. You can write about 20 lines on a screen. If you need to send more information, use an attachment.

Do use e-mail to reduce telephone and meeting time.

Don't use e-mail for all communication. It's impersonal. You can't see the other person's facial expression or body language, or hear their voice. Sometimes you need to make a phone call or meet in person.

Don't expect an answer right away. E-mail messages may be delivered quickly, but your recipient needs time to consider your message and decide how to respond.

Don't send a message several times. Your recipient won't appreciate it.

Tip Remember that e-mail sent from work is not private. Companies can and do monitor both work-related and private messages that are sent on company time. Keep romances, gossip, and company secrets off the net.

We often irritate others when we think we could not possibly do so.

—La Rochefoucauld

Part 20

Bringing it all together—making a million dollar first impression

Always be a first rate version
of yourself instead of a
second rate version of
someone else.
—Judy Garland

101. How to make sure others perceive you the way you want them to

Have you heard this story?

A famous person is at a fancy restaurant. The famous person asks the server for extra butter. The server answers, "Sorry, only one pat of butter per customer." The famous person becomes indignant, and asks, "Do you know who I am?" The server answers, "No, I don't. Who are you?"

The famous person explains all the amazing things he has done, and says, "Now will you bring me some more butter?" "Sorry, I can't," says the server. "Do you know who I am?"

"No," admits the famous person. "Who are you?"

"I'm the person in charge of the butter," the server replies.

This story shows that your image is created by the way people perceive you. This is based on how you project yourself. Even if you are "only in charge of the butter," do the very best you can, in whatever you are doing. Your image will reflect your confidence, and demand respect.

102. Why you have to sell yourself over and over again

In your parents' or grandparents' generation people may have worked at the same job for most of their lives, and retired with the "golden handshake." Not any more. The trend for the future is working at a series of different jobs. We may change companies, or even careers, several times during our lifetimes. This means that we have to continually sell ourselves to new companies and clients.

If selling yourself sounds like something your mother taught you never to do, think again. We all sell our ideas, and ourselves, whether we realize it or not. Teachers sell their ideas to their students. Teenagers sell the idea of staying out later to their parents. Kids figure out, at a very young age, how to sell their parents on what they want. You know how to do this naturally, too.

Our ability to sell ourselves determines our success or failure in business. We always have to make sure our expertise, knowledge and business acumen are visible. You want the world to see your professionalism, your enthusiasm for the job, and your interest in the person or company.

Being an executive recruiter, I naturally expect a certain level of savvy, and professional etiquette from my candidates. Our company has the privilege of interviewing the cream of the crop, however, there are still things that make these high-powered individuals stand apart from others; an unintimidating, unpretentious sense of power. Yes, the aura of power. The greatness from within, that radiates outwardly as confidence, approachability, or poise. It stems from knowing who you are, where you are going, and WHY.

—Andrea Bruderer, Vice President, SB Personnel

103. Why we use the 85/15 formula to make decisions

How do you make buying decisions? Do you read consumer reports, or ask the store clerk detailed questions? Maybe for big-ticket items, but a large part of your decision is probably based on what you like. Most of us even make major purchases like cars, based mainly on color and style. Surprised? Successful sales people aren't.

Sure, we read the statistics and information, but our final decision is often based more on emotion than logic. In fact, statistics show that our decisions are based 85 percent on emotion, and 15 percent on logic. Then we use statistics to back up our decisions.

How does the 85/15 percent formula relate to you? Someone who likes you will trust you, and will want to do business with you. How do you get them to like you? By smiling, greeting them warmly,—in other words, all the things that make a positive first impression.

That's right. A great first impression is really an emotional reaction. Of course you need good job skills. But if you neglect the people skills, you will have trouble making the emotional connection you need to land the job, contract or client you want. Remember, people make decisions based on their emotions. Make sure they connect emotionally with you.

104. Why you should fake it until you make it

We all have inner pictures of ourselves. We may have learned, over the years, to become overly self-critical. But if we hold on to that vision of ourselves and cultivate it, others will perceive us in a negative way.

To succeed in business, the most important ingredient is self-confidence. How do you gain confidence if you don't have much? Simply by learning how confident people act. For example, you know that successful people make eye contact. You can learn to do the same thing. You have to practice your new skills until they become real.

The amazing part is that, as you practice your new techniques, people will perceive you as confident, and react to you as a confident person. This will further help build your self-esteem. After a while, these new habits become second nature, and you will realize that you actually feel more confident.

golden nugget 18 When you act the way you want to be, you will soon become that way.

105. Why the 12-second factor applies to retail packages and to you

The "12 second factor" is a concept in retail sales. It means that a sales person has 12 seconds to capture a buyer's attention with the product's design, packaging and position.

It works for us too. You may have only seconds to make a powerful first impression, but that's all you really need. Your appearance, actions and language come across immediately. They should reflect your confidence and professionalism.

Use the first 12 seconds to open the door. Then you will have time to show your talents and abilities, so people will want to pursue a business relationship with you. To do this, you don't have to assume a new personality, or have plastic surgery. You just have to be your personal best. Focus on your strongest abilities, your key features. Practice the techniques in this book. Then you'll be on the road to making a million dollar first impression.

There are three people I can think of that truly left me with a lasting professional impression over the course of the years. They all possessed the same qualities: confidence and calm. They were all good listeners, and would intensely gaze into your eyes when you spoke. When you'd finish, they would speak calmly and confidently, with wisdom beyond their years.

—Sandy Thompson, Regional Director (Independent Representative), Excel Communications

After meeting a person for the first time, I continue to think of them in a special way if they have touched my soul and inspired me by who they are, rather than by what they do for a living.

—Andrea Strom-Rancourt, M.A.
President, Live Well International

Summary of Golden Nuggets

1. Your physical appearance is your visual resume.

2. Of all the things you wear, your facial expression is the most important.

3. Your body language speaks louder than the words you say.

4. Extend your hand to anyone you are doing business with—male or female.

5. Say the name of the most honored person first in business introductions. Remember that the client is always the most important person in a business relationship.

6. Use someone's name to show you value them.

7. Follow the same rules for men and women in today's gender-neutral business arena.

8. Your business card represents your professional image. Make sure it's a "keeper."

9. The small details of your image complete the big picture.

10. Dress for the job you aspire to, not the job you have now.

11. You will always project a polished, professional image with a classic, up-to-date look.
12. The reason for a business meal is building relationships. The setting is the restaurant.
13. Networking connects you with people who can help you reach your business goals.
14. Make a memorable introduction within 60 seconds using a USP.
15. Small talk is important because it leads to big talk.
16. Your first impression on the telephone may be the only one you get to make.
17. Use your business correspondence to make a permanent, professional impression.
18. When you act the way you want to be, you will soon become that way.

Sample Letter Format
Block Style

Company Letterhead

(five spaces after letterhead)

18 September 2002

Mr. John Smith
Business Title
Company Name
2654 Main Street
Winnipeg MB M3T 5X4

Dear Mr. Smith:

This is a sample of a block style business letter. A business letter is written on letterhead paper. It follows the format you see here.

Be sure the letter is clear, concise and uses paragraphs. Ideally a business letter is on one page. It includes a complimentary close.

Sincerely,

Jane White
Business title

Sample Letter Format
Modified Block Style

Company Letterhead

(five spaces after letterhead)

12 January 2002

Mr. John Smith
Business Title
Company Name
2654 Main Street
Winnipeg MB M3T 5X4

Dear Mr. Smith:

This is a sample of a modified block style business letter. It is written on letterhead paper. The date and complimentary close are on the right and paragraphs are indented.

The body of the letter is clear, concise and uses paragraphs. Ideally a business letter is on one page. It includes a complimentary close.

Sincerely,

Jane White
Business title

Sample Memo Format

MEMORANDUM

TO: All Staff Members

FROM: Jane White, General Manager

DATE: 10 December 2003

SUBJECT: Report on Memo Format

Memo is the term used in spoken English. The written form is memorandum. The word memorandum appears in capital letters to the left at the top of the memo.

Memos follow the format you see in this sample. Memos are not signed, but they may be followed by the sender's hand-written initials at the left margin.

Sample FAX Cover Sheet

Company Letterhead

To:	John Smith, Director of Marketing
Fax:	(604) 457-8759
From:	Jane Jones, Accountant
Fax:	(514) 271-9384
Date:	20 September 2001
Pages:	4 pages including the cover sheet. If all pages are not received, call (514) 271- 8657.
Subject:	**Proposal for Markcting Budget for January 2002**

Message: We will be discussing the marketing budget for next year at our meeting in Calgary. Your feedback will be welcome at that time.

Index

Order Form

Give the gift of business success

How to Make a Million Dollar First Impression is the perfect gift for anyone in the business world.

Order securely online : www.Impressforsuccess.com
and receive a FREE booklet, "Business Casual, or Business Casualty?"

Quantity discounts available for bulk purchases.

Please rush me _______ copies of *How to Make a Million Dollar First Impression* at 15.95 US or $19.95 Canadian (GST included), plus $4.50 shipping/book.

Quantity	Unit Price	Shipping & Handling	Total

My check or money order for $____ is enclosed.
Name ______________________________

Address ______________________________

City/Province/State ______________________________

Country /Postal/Zip ______________________________

Phone: Home ____________ Business ____________

Please make your check payable and return to
Goldman Seminars
2216 Mediterranée
ST-Laurent, Quebec
Canada H4R 3B1

How can we help you succeed?

We offer customized seminars and workshops to help you feel confident in any business situation. We work with corporations, associations, business schools and entrepreneurs to provide tools for your success.

Lynda Goldman is a business image consultant, seminar leader and writer. Her newspaper column, "First Impressions," magazine articles, and e-zine, "Business Image Tips" provide ongoing tips for success. Lynda Goldman and Sandra Smythe Thibaudeau are authors of 27 best-selling books, and business consultants for more than 10 years.

Call us to find out about our seminars on business dining and receptions, first impressions and business image, and receive a free consultation about your needs.

Lynda Goldman, Goldman Smythe & Associates
Your Premiere Business Image & Etiquette Resource

Phone: (514) 336-4339
Fax: (514) 336-9805
Toll-free: 1-877-462-4384
E-mail: Lyndag@goldmansmythe.com

Free e-mail newsletter, "Business Image Tips" at: www.goldmansmythe.com Free report for signing up: 10 Tips for Better E-mail Etiquette